Essays on African-Centered Psychology

Restoring the African Mind Research Collection

1 THE LIMITS OF EUROCENTRIC PSYCHOLOGY

In critiquing what he referred to as "Eurocentric psychology" Amos Wilson explained that "while offering us some information of value" he also felt "that this approach is inadequate: primarily because it appears to be relatively non-political." By contrast, Wilson notes that "Black psychology is openly and consciously political and recognizes that the very basis for what we might call mental problems, or other kinds of problems in the Black community, is the political structure […]." Wilson is essentially arguing that whereas white psychologists tended to approach psychology from a non-political or politically neutral perspective, black psychologists were often more overtly political in their study of psychology.

Before delving into the topic of Eurocentric psychology versus Black psychology, the limitations of a strictly non-political approach to psychology should be addressed. In "The Politics of Abnormal Psychology: Past, Present, and Future," Isaac Prilleltensky makes the case for a more consciously political approach to psychology. He explains that one major flaw in the study of abnormal psychology is the "defect method" which analyzes "inappropriate" behavior as being part of "an internal organic or psychological malfunction." In other words, the abnormality of a person is considered to be inherent to that individual and environmental factors on behavior are considered secondary. Of this model Prilleltensky writes: "Inadvertently, the defect paradigm promoted the notion that maladapted persons are the sole product of a less able organism and/or a genetic handicap. As a result, preventive social action is not deemed crucial."

Prilleltensky also writes about "community psychology" which attempts to locate human behavior within the wider context of global forces such as the economy and politics, but Prilleltensky argues that this approach falls short because community psychologists do not challenge the political status quo:

> The unequal distribution of power in society and its concomitant fragmentation into markedly opposed interest groups. That is to say that in principle community

psychology promotes the politicization of abnormal behavior, a much-needed emphasis. However, when they become involved in the political arena, the kind of politics advocated by community psychologists is not a radical one. In other words, it is a politics that does not threaten the status quo. Consequently, its implications are not as effectual as desired. An elaboration of these propositions is in order.

Based on this we can see that one of the clear limitations of an approach to psychology that is strictly non-political is that it fails to assess the often political roots of certain maladaptive behaviors in individuals. In many cases, to improve such behaviors would require fundamental social changes. Prilleltensky concludes:

> Countless obstacles will be encountered by those willing to invigorate the field of abnormal psychology by entering the turbulent political scene of community life. Psychologists prepared to give up some of the comfort afforded by the scientist-professional model to question existing social structures are likely to risk severe opposition from their employing institutions, as well as isolation from colleagues who may perceive their activities as derogating the painfully gained scientific reputation of psychology. This embroilment is occasioned by a model whose chief goal is the promotion of human welfare, as opposed to paradigms designed primarily to dissect the human experience in the hope of finding replicable laws of behavior. The latter may be conducted without disrupting the social order. The former is bound to perturb the status quo.

It should also be remembered that white psychologists operated in a white dominated society and very rarely did they feel the need to challenge that racial status quo. In fact, white psychologists at times contributed to White Supremacy by putting forward notions that African people were mentally inferior to Europeans. G. Stanley Hall, who founded the *American Journal of Psychology* and served as the first president of the American Psychological Association, wrote:

> Certain primitive races are in a state of immature development and must be treated gently and understandingly by more developed peoples. Africans, Indians and Chinese are members of adolescent races in a stage of incomplete development.

Carl Jung expressed a similar view when he argued that Africans have "probably a whole historical layer less (in the collective unconscious) than you (Caucasians). The different strata of the mind correspond to the history of the races." Very rarely did white psychologists feel the need to address racism, or any aspect of the social structure for that matter. This is to say that very rarely did the work of notable psychologists take on a political context or attempt to challenge the status quo of their time. Sigmund Freud was concerned with understanding the unconscious desires of the human mind. John B. Watson was concerned with understanding human behavior. Abraham Maslow's focus was on his concept of self-actualization. None of them made a conscious decision to use their work to challenge oppressive aspects of the existing status quo.

Carl Rogers stands out as somewhat of an exception to the notable white psychologists in the field. He was very vocal on some of the political issues of his time. One of which was McCarthyism, which was initiated to subvert communist sympathizers in the United States. When the University of Chicago's laboratory school was threatened, Rogers wrote a letter which read:

> You feel that the solution for this situation is discipline by authority—giving up the democratic attempt. I can think of no better way of undermining the already badly shaken democratic philosophy of this country than to move the elementary schools in the direction of a more authoritarian philosophy. My own experience in working with individuals and groups leads me to believe that the solution

lies in a direction which is diametrically opposed to yours. I feel the solution is to work toward a real democracy in our schools, with each individual genuinely participating in responsible choices. I would replace "democratic rituals" with real democracy rather than with authoritarianism. I would aim for responsible self-discipline, not for discipline imposed by "legitimate authority."

In 1956, Rogers participated in a debate with B.F. Skinner. In this debate he warned about the danger of the government using behavioral science to control their citizens:

It is my hope that we have helped to clarify the range of choice which will lie before us and our children in regard to the behavioral sciences. We can choose to use our growing knowledge to enslave people in ways never dreamed of before, depersonalizing them, controlling them by means so carefully selected that they will perhaps never be aware of their loss of personhood. We can choose to utilize our scientific knowledge to make men happy, well-behaved, and productive, as Skinner earlier suggested. Or we can insure that each person learns all the syllabus which we select and set before him, as Skinner now suggests. Or at the other end of the spectrum of choice we can choose to use the behavioral sciences in ways which will free, not control; which will develop creativity, not contentment; which will facilitate each person in his self-directed process of becoming; which will aid individuals, groups, and even the concept of science to become self-transcending in freshly adaptive ways of meeting life and its problems.

Rogers expressed a deep concern over the potential development of authoritarian practices on the part of the American government. Rogers himself was never a political figure, however. This is to say that Rogers was not an activist of any sort. He may have questioned aspects of McCarthyism, but the critique of McCarthyism never became an important part of his work as a psychologist, nor did Rogers attempt to directly challenge such undemocratic practices of McCarthyism. The most overt political work that Rogers engaged in was his work with the Central Intelligence Agency (CIA). Rogers was motivated to work with the CIA by the politics of the Cold War between America and Russia. Rogers explained: "It seemed as though Russia was a very potential enemy and as though the United States was very wise to get whatever information it could about things that the Russians might try to do, such as brainwashing or influencing people. So that it didn't seem at all dishonorable to me to be connected with an intelligence outfit at that time. I look at it quite differently now."

Erich Fromm also stands out as an even more political figure than Rogers was. Fromm, who was born in Germany, left the country after the Nazis came to power. He moved to the United States where he joined the Socialist Party of America and challenged McCarthyism. Rogers and Fromm were two white psychologists whose work did take on a political significance in some regards, but generally speaking most of the prominent white psychologists who emerged in the field were not very politically active.

Psychologists of African descent have used their work to not only study the things that psychologists have typically studied such as behavior or the subconscious, but some have used their work to challenge the status quo and fight for real social and political change—this is what Wilson was referring to when he distinguished between Black psychology and Eurocentric psychology. They have not only focused on abnormal behavior or maladaptive behavior within the African community, but they have also looked at the socio-political environment that people of African descent live in and have worked to change that environment to create changes in the behaviors of African people. One of the best examples of this in the United States are Kenneth and Mamie Clark, whose doll tests were instrumental in the *Brown v. Board of Education* case which ruled that segregated education was unconstitutional. The Clarks' psychological experiment contributed to changing the laws of America because the test demonstrated that the policy of segregated education had an adverse psychological impact on children of African descent.

The influence of the Clarks on the civil rights movement went beyond that experiment. Together they developed Harlem Youth Opportunities Unlimited (HARYOU) as an organization to assist African Americans with education and employment opportunities. Kenneth Clark also hosted a program called *Three Perspectives* in which he interviewed Malcolm X, Martin Luther King, and James Baldwin, discussing with them their perspectives on the civil rights movement.

2 ON THE LEGACY OF EDNA ROLAND

Edna Maria Santos Roland, a social psychologist and Brazilian activist, provides perhaps the most extensive example of the political nature of Black Psychology because of her lifelong activism. Roland began her activism not against racism, but as a member of the student movements in Brazil that protested the military government that was in power at the time. Roland did not become involved in the African struggles against racism until the 1980s, during the period of Brazil's return to democracy.

Roland was born in northeast Brazil, but migrated throughout Brazil for most of her childhood and adolescence. Roland grew up in a middle class family, which afforded her many opportunities. Her family also stressed the importance of education. At the age of 16, Roland left for the United States to study as an exchange student. It was there that she would discover her identity, as she explained:

> During a trip to the USA, I was in a bus with only white children and parked next to it was a bus with only black children. We heard a blast that sounded like a bomb, and the white students in my bus went into panic and then I realized that they were afraid because the other students were black. And I was also afraid of those black students, so I stopped to reflect…Who am I? What am I? And so I immediately began to question my own ethnic identity. In my childhood I had faced some discrimination within the family with relation to my white friends, but that did not raise my awareness. The moment of revelation was during that incident in the USA. It was exactly at that moment that I realized my own discrimination and racism, and begin asking questions about my identity.

It was during these years of military dictatorship that Roland became involved in political organizations when she joined the student movement. The military repression forced her to cut ties with her family, her university, and abandon her post-graduate studies. Throughout the 1970s Roland's actions were aimed towards the issue of the military government and the restoration of democracy in Brazil, but she eventually became involved in the fight for the rights of African people in Brazil.

The fight for African liberation gained some momentum in the 1940s and 1950s, with the creation of the Frente Negra Brasileira (Black Brazilian Front). Unfortunately this party was shut down by President Vargas, when he declared Brazil a one-party state and made all other political organizations illegal. With the restoration of democracy in 1985, a number of social movements began to reappear again. One of the black organizations to emerge during this period was the Unified Black Movement, (Movimento Negro Unificado) (MNU). In the early 1980s, Roland tried to get involved with the MNU, but was unsuccessful. Roland did become involved in the cultural aspects of the black movement in the '80s, however. She took part in African groups that paraded during carnival.

Since the 1980s, Roland has been on the forefront of the fight against racism in Brazil. Roland was one of the founders of the *Geledés Instituto da Mulher Negra* (Geledés Institute of the Black Woman), which was founded in 1988. She was also a founder of *Fala Preta* (Black Voice) and became president of this organization in 1997. An article that was written in celebration of Geledés' 25th anniversary described the organization as follows:

> Geledés is a black women's organization whose institutional mission is to fight racism and sexism, value and promote African-descendent women in particular, and the African-descendent community in general. Its objective is to increase the visibility of the racial problem in Brazil and to make the government and civil society more sensitive to the discussion of the growing exclusionary process faced by the poor and discriminated populations constituted mainly by African-descendents.

Geledés was formed to, as Sueli Carnerio explained, "blacken feminism." African feminists found that within the feminist movement in Brazil there was little consideration for the issue of racism and other struggles that African women faced. Roland argued that African women in Brazil were oppressed three times: for being African, for being poor, and for being a woman. Activists such as Roland realized that no existing organization in Brazil effectively dealt with the often intersecting issues of racism, sexism, and poverty in Brazil. This is what Geledés was founded to address.

Geledés was just one of a number of organizations for Afro-Brazilian women that emerged in the 1980s. Of Geledés and similar organizations Roland explained:

> The importance that has been given to our problems today is much greater than it was, for example, six years ago, six or seven years ago, when Geledés was created. Today, it is no longer possible for a large encounter to take place, for a large conference to take place—whether about blacks or about women—that does not give the question of the black woman a large political space that is given a separate place of importance. This is something that Geledés along with other groups of black women in Brazil achieved.

The word Geledés itself carries much significance for African women. It refers to a custom in Yoruba society which honors female elders, ancestors, and deities. The custom was meant to express female power. This is not only significant for empowering African women in Brazil, but also because of its attempt to utilize aspects of African culture to assist in the struggles of the African Diaspora in Brazil. In order to empower African women in Brazil, the organization draws on an African tradition which was empowering for women.

Geledés was involved in a number of important developments in the African struggle in Brazil. Among them was initiating a dialogue with the Hip Hop Movement in São Paulo, with the intent of fostering an interest in discussing racial issues among the leaders of the movement. Geledés developed a health program to address issues such as reproductive health and AIDs. Roland served as the Health Director in Geledés. Geledés also worked with SOS Racismo to provide legal services to victims of racial discrimination and Geledés played an important role in the formation of *Articulação de Mulheres Negras Brasileiras*

(Articulation of Brazilian Black Women). Geledés' work has also expanded beyond Brazil. In 1994, Geledés initiated a dialogue with other African organizations in South America. From this eventually came the *Aliança Estratégica de Organizações Negras da América Latina e Caribe* (Strategic Alliance of Black Organizations of Latin America and the Caribbean).

Aside from her work with various organizations in Brazil, Roland has also worked with the United Nations to address racism.

In 2001, Roland attended the World Conference on Racism, Racial Discrimination, Xenophobia and Related Intolerance in Durban, South Africa. On this occasion she was appointed as a speaker of the conference. In this capacity she, and other Brazilian activists, raised the issue of reparations for the descendants of enslaved Africans living outside of Africa. The conference also formed a consensus on using the term Afro-descendent to describe the descendants of enslaved Africans. Roland explained that "Durban was a watershed experience for the Brazilian Black Power Movement," because it was this meeting that forced the Brazilian government to revise its discourse on racial democracy. No longer could the government deny the existence of racism in Brazil after this conference. To demonstrate the extent to which the conference in South Africa changed the public discourse on race in Brazil, the Minister of Education Paulo Renato Souza wrote a letter addressing the topic of affirmative action; a topic which was previously considered taboo in Brazil.

The news that Roland, a psychologist, had been made a rapporteur for the conference in Durban was a surprise to other psychologists in Brazil, as well as a source of pride. Although Roland is a psychologist by profession, Roland also described herself as an activist of the black movement and an activist in the struggle for human rights in Brazil. Roland was one of the many activists who opposed the military dictatorship in Brazil.

Through her work with the United Nations, Roland was able to advocate not only for reparations, but also for policies which address the problem of racism against African people in Brazil. Much of Roland's organizing activities have also centered around the U.N.'s efforts to address racism. The U.N. declared the

International Decade for People of African Descent, which began in 2015. One of the activities which the Coordination of Racial Equality of the Prefecture of Guarulhos—of which Roland was involved in—organized for the International Decade of People of African Descent was a march against racism which was organized to take place every year on November 20th, which is Black Awareness Day in Brazil. Black Awareness Day is a day which honors the rebel leader Zumbi. Roland also participated in the inauguration of AFROMADRID, which was organized in 2015 for the International Decade for People of African Descent.

Roland also appeared on a program with Congresswoman Ana Alencar to discuss the Special Secretariat for the Promotion of Racial Equality which was created by the government of Brazil for the purpose of participating in discussions regarding the Racial Equality Statute. The program discussed the International Day for the End of Racial Discrimination on March 21. This day was created by the U.N. to commemorate the Sharpeville Massacre in South Africa. The Secretariat for the Promotion of Racial Equality in Brazil decided to extend the commemoration of this occasion until March 25.

Roland acknowledged that the abovementioned statute was conceived based on the problems confronting African people in Brazil, but she explained: "This does not mean that any other social group that is the victim of discrimination does not deserve attention from public policies. But it is necessary for us to pay attention to the specifics of the problem of each racial ethnic group." For Roland, this meant that the indigenous peoples must also be guaranteed their rights as well.

In 2003, Roland was nominated as an "eminent specialist" by the Secretary General of the United Nations to monitor the implementation of resolutions relating to racism in Latin America. Roland also wrote a report for the UN relating to racism in Latin America, which was compiled in *United to Combat Racism*. In this report Roland provides an overview of the struggles of African people throughout South America and the Caribbean based on the reports that each country provided to the Elimination of all Forms of Racial Discrimination (ICERD) concerning their efforts at eliminating racism.

In the overview Roland notes that many South American nations do not collect data on racial backgrounds, so that the population of African descent is "drastically underestimated" in the Western hemisphere. Roland mentions the specific example of Colombia, where the government claimed that Afro-Colombians made up 16% of the population, whereas the Departamento Nacional de Planeación claimed that Afro-Colombians made up 56% of the population. One of the problematic aspects of determining the number of people of African descent in South America is the history of "whitening" in the region. Roland explains that the "small proportion of Europeans determined the manipulation of race classification in such a way that people would be perceived as 'passing' to a lighter tone: a pigmentocracy was built so that one's hierarchical position would be determined in relation to the darkness of one's skin." The result of this has been the development of the concept of "racial democracy" which was built on the idea of hybridism. Roland argues that the ideal of racial democracy disguises "the violence, the roughness, the fierceness under which the so-called mixing of races occurred."

The creation of this "pigmentocracy" was useful for maintaining white domination in South America, where whites were often outnumbered by both the indigenous and African population. Consistent with the goal of "whitening", many South American countries have taken steps to render the African population invisible. One of the ways this was done is through the census, in which no information on racial backgrounds was collected. Roland points out that "the absence of information has been instrumental in the production of a European and a Mestizo image of certain parts of Latin America [...]."

Roland points out that the attempts to address racism in the region have excluded Africans. The National Institute to Combat Discrimination, Xenophobia and Racism was created to provide reparation for moral and material damages from discrimination. The report that was presented by Argentina concentrated on discrimination against indigenous groups and Jews, but only one case relating to an African was mentioned. In its 13th report to the Committee on Elimination of Racial Discrimination, Bolivia made no reference to Afro-Bolivians. Chile's 14th periodic report mentioned racial discrimination relating to indigenous groups. Africans were only mentioned once as "African immigrants" who came during the colonial period and "have been absorbed in the general miscegenation." Roland details the various disparities in Brazil between the African and white population. Roland then explains that important issues such as "access to land, education at all levels and especially at university level, access to higher grade jobs, access to capital, equity in the justice system, adequate housing" all remained to be confronted by the government.

The position of the Dominican Republic was a defensive one. They claimed that there was no existence of racism and claimed that the whole thing was merely an excuse for non-governmental organizations to exist. The Dominican Republic also asserted that the thousands of Haitians that were forced to leave returned the next day as an example of the non-discrimination against Haitians. The report of Panama was similarly troubling in its misrepresentation of the situation in the country. Their 10th and 14th reports recognized that members of the African and Asian minorities did not benefit from the rights that were protected by ICERD. The report referred to Africans as a minority group, but the Comunidades de Ancestria Africana estimated that as much as 77% of Panama's population was of African descent. Roland also mentions the influence that Marcus Garvey had on Panamanian workers, as well as the adverse impact that America's invasion of Panama had on Afro-Panamanians. Paraguay did not ratify ICERD and there were few studies done about Afro-Paraguayans.

Roland ends this report with a list of recommendations for policies that could be implemented to help eliminate racism from the region. This included reparations for the damages caused by racism:

> Afro-Americans must be assured just and adequate reparation for material and moral damage suffered as a result of racial discrimination. Reparations, be they monetary or non-monetary should have sufficient coercive or persuasive power to discourage the occurrence of the offence. Appropriate laws, access to court, and adequate training of the judiciary power on the national and

international instruments of protection related to racial discrimination, xenophobia, ethnic violence and related intolerance are key issues to combat racism and to assure the economic, social and cultural rights of Afro-Americans.

Roland also delivered a statement in 2011 in honor of the 10th anniversary of the adoption of the Durban Declaration and Programme of Action. Roland noted some important steps that came out of the meeting, such as Latin American nations that have included Africans in their census, which has helped increase representation for the previously neglected African communities. Despite the advancements, Roland also noted continued problems such as discrimination and violence. Roland described the deaths of Africans and indigenous youth as being "a situation that has been considered genocide." At the time that Roland gave this address, Africans in Chile were campaigning to be counted on the 2012 census, so there were still nations where Africans were not represented on the official census.

Roland is a psychologist, but in her struggle against racism she has worked as a political activist both within local organizations and with the UN. Roland and the other black psychologists that have been mentioned here stand out as psychologists who challenged the racist status quos of the societies that they lived in. These psychologists recognized that traditional approaches to the study of psychology—approaches which were developed by people of European descent, some of which were themselves racists—were inadequate for dealing with the psychological challenges of African people because so many of those challenges had political roots and therefore required political solutions.

3 THE DEBATE OVER AFRICAN HISTORY

The European assault on African people was a brutal one. During slavery, colonization, Jim Crow, apartheid, and all of the other systematic forms of racism and oppression African people were brutalized, raped, lynched, burned alive, buried alive, castrated, beheaded, whipped, mutilated, and suffered many other forms of physical violence. What also went into this oppression was the stripping of the very identity of African people through the robbing of their history. On the slave plantations African people were stripped of their languages, names, cultural practices, and religion. Those Africans who attempted to maintain their language or culture were brutally punished. Olaudah Equiano recalled that he was renamed Gustavus Vassa and when he refused to acknowledge his new name he was beaten until he submitted.

Africans were forced to adjust to a society that was hostile and contrary to the society that they knew. Whereas African societies tended to be family orientated, life for Africans on the slave plantations was the opposite. Husbands and wives, parents and children, grandparents and grand-children, were all separated from each other on a regular basis. Therefore, the very lifestyles of African people were altered on the slave plantations. This contributed to the fracturing of the identities of African people.

Robbing African people of their sense of self served two major purposes. One of which was making African more docile and less rebellious. This was so effective that many Africans refused to run away from the plantations even when given the opportunity to do so. Harriet Tubman often carried a pistol with her not only for self-defense, but to threaten those who wanted to return to the plantations after having left. The other purpose of this robbing of the self-identity of African people was that by reinforcing this idea that African people were an inferior and savage people with no history Europeans also justified their own mistreatment of African people.

The erasing of history played a critical role in approaches to the academic study of African history, especially as it related to Egypt. Marcus Garvey (1923) pointed out that white historians flat out denied the racial identity of the Egyptians:

The white world has always tried to rob and discredit us of our history. They tell us that Tut-Ankh-Amen, a King of Egypt, who reigned about the year 1350 B. C. (before Christ), was not a Negro, that the ancient civilization of Egypt and the Pharaohs was not of our race, but that does not make the truth unreal.

Garvey's statement should be elaborated on a bit more given the fact that the debate over the identity of the Egyptians best exemplifies the extent that Western scholars have gone to discredit African history or to deny African people their rightful place in history. It should be made clear from the onset that a very popular tactic used to discredit African history has been to ascribe any achievements in Africa to outside influences. An example of this was the civilization of Great Zimbabwe in Africa. Its historical achievements were attributed to Phoenicians to avoid giving credit to African people. This view was challenged by Peter Garlake. This brought Garlake into conflict with Ian Smith's government. Smith hired individuals to challenge Garlake's conclusions. Garlake was forced into exile in 1970 simply for daring to write the truth about the history of Great Zimbabwe. In an obituary for Garlake titled "Peter Garlake (1934-2011), Great Zimbabwe and the politics of the past in Zimbabwe," Innocent Pikirayi wrote that "Peter Garlake enjoyed considerable international recognition for the high quality and impact of his recent research, all of which indicated his standing as a leading international scholar." This was also precisely why the government of Rhodesia opposed his work.

W.E.B. Du Bois dismissed the idea that the culture of West Africa was anything but native when he writes: "Effort has naturally been made to ascribe this civilization to white people. First it was ascribed to Portuguese influence, but much of it is evidently older than the Portuguese discovery, Egypt and India have been evoked and Greece and Carthage. But all these explanations are far-fetched. If ever a people exhibited unanswerable evidence of indigenous civilization, it is the west-coast Africans. Undoubtedly they adapted much that came to them, utilized new ideas, and grew from contact. But their art and culture is Negro through and through."

The attempting at suppressing African history was not merely about suppressing knowledge about historical events and personalities. It is deeper than this. In his book, The Falsification of Afrikan Consciousness, Amos Wilson explained, "We, as individuals, are our history." He states:

> If you forgot your past you would not be able to understand me right now. You would not be able to walk or talk. You did not learn to walk, and talk and do the things you're doing at the moment when you entered here; you learned to them in the past.

The repression of history also creates what Wilson terms "historical and experiential amnesia." This is to say that history contains problem solving abilities and the loss of that history creates a loss of "access to crucially important social, intellectual and technical skills associated with that history which could be used to resolve current problems." For this reason Wilson points out that historical amnesia can handicap the person or group suffering from it. In his "Message to the Grassroots" speech, Malcolm X explained the importance of history for problem solving: "Of all our studies, history is best qualified to reward our research. And when you see that you've got problems, all you have to do is examine the historic method used all over the world by others who have problems similar to yours. And once you see how they got theirs straight, then you know how you can get yours straight."

Wilson continues by explaining that history plays a very important role in the oppression of a people. Wilson explains:

> History is real; it brings real, tangible results. When we wish to negate it and not integrate it, when we wish to negate it and not affirm it, then it negates us in the end. The negation wins out. The Afrikan person who lives in social amnesia brought on by the projection of mythological Eurocentric history, lives a life that is unintegrated and misunderstood.

A lack of understanding of history also leads to a lack of understanding of one's own actions, as Wilson explains:

> Consequently, when the European makes us unconscious of our own history, we not only become unconscious of our history as knowledge, we become unconscious of the sources of our behavior as persons and as a people; and our own behavior becomes a mystery. "Why do Black-folks act like that?" We get discouraged.

So in studying and understanding one's history we also come to find the roots of particular problems, as well as the solutions or frameworks for developing solutions for those problems. Therefore history cannot be merely dismissed as something that happened in the past and has no real relevance to the lives of people in the present. History forms the very basis for the present and in the case of African people, history forms the very framework for which we strive towards finding solutions to the problems that we face.

Amos Wilson offered a specific example of what he referred as tontines (also known as susu). In 1987, the *New York Times* ran a story on banking in Cameroon. The story stated: "When Samuel Nanci needed $35,000 to open his Joie de Vivre Bar here, he did not bother with banks. Instead he turned to the tontines, an informal credit system rooted in African tradition. Without signing a paper or filling out a form, Mr. Nanci emerged from his monthly tontine meeting with $35,000 in cash."

Economists predicted that African tontines would die out with the rise of modern economies that were based on European banking systems, but this was not the case. Theodoret-Marie Fansi, the director of an economic consulting firm in Cameroon, explained that banks do not match the mentality of the people. He described them as "colonial structures." This structure was so alien to the people that loan delinquency rates were as high as 50 percent in Cameroon. The report states: "Tontines work, economists say, because their loans are backed by social *pressure*, a system familiar to Africans. Banks perform poorly because their loans are backed by paper guarantees made to strangers, a concept alien to

Africans."

The social pressure of the tontine system was so great that borrowers were known to commit suicide when faced with delinquency. Those who failed to pay off their loan faced being rejected by the community. It was this social pressure—the threat of being rejected by the community—that drove people to pay back money borrowed from tontines. This also speaks to the fact that economic systems are not only about where you spend your money, but how people within that system relate to each other. Some Africans really embrace this idea of individualism, yet when we look at European history we find that Europeans have not just oppressed us as individuals, but within a collective system. Jim Crow and apartheid, for example, were institutionalized systems of racism. We do not make collective progress through individual action. An African economic system recognizes this.

Susu operates in the same way that the tontines of Cameroon does. This is an informal loan in which a group of people contributes a total sum of money. Each time the group meets a different person within the group receives the sum of money. This is done until every member of the group receives the contributed sum of money. Say for example, a group of ten people decide to meet biweekly and each member contributes $100 at every meeting. The group would meet ten times until each member receives the $100 payout. Many Caribbean people that have migrated to the United States used the susu system to establish businesses of their own, buy houses, or send their children to college. This is a system of informally giving out loans which survived the Middle Passage and slavery. It is also a system which proves to be very effective at raising large sums of money in a short space of time. Moreover, unlike Western capitalist forms of banking, susus involve no interest rates or fees.

The traditional justice system of the Acholi/Luo in Uganda gives us a detailed example of a traditional African judicial system and another example of the practical application of African history. In Uganda, the Lord's Resistance Army (LRA) led by Joseph Kony, was known for committing all sorts of atrocities. Their campaign to overthrow the government and replace it with a regime based on the Ten Commandments became a campaign that involved massacring and mutilating the civilian population. They also abducted children and used them as soldiers.

It was decided that for the war to end all those who committed the atrocities had to be forgiven. LRA rebels were given full amnesty. The community used traditional cleansing and forgiveness rituals. This traditional judicial system is known as Mato Oput (reconciliation). Of Mato Oput, Rev. Mcleod Baker Ochola states:

> If capital punishment were deemed appropriate for such offender, he/she is kept in isolation and confinement, as a wrong and dangerous element to the community or society. If it is life imprisonment, the offender would be put out of circulation from the larger society for ever. This is meant to serve justice for the victims and/or survivors of the offence. Presumably, it is also supposed to serve justice for the society at large as some form of deterrence. But have these forms of punishment succeeded to expand justice and reduce crimes?

The story behind the creation of Mato Oput is an interesting one. According to oral tradition the practice of Mato Oput traces back to the separation of two brothers named Labongo and Gipir. In Luo society the spear is not only a weapon, but also a symbol of power, authority, and leadership. Labongo, being the elder son, was given the ancestral spear by his elderly father. During the ceremony, Labongo was made to swear on his ancestors that he would guard the ancestral spear with his life.

One morning an elephant wandered into a garden of cowpeas that belonged to Labongo. Labongo was away hunting at the time, but Gipir was made aware of the elephant and rushed to protect the garden. In a hurry, Labongo grabbed the ancestral spear and threw the spear at the elephant, wounding the creature. The elephant ran away with the spear still stuck in it. It was only after the elephant escaped that Gipir realized what he had done. Labongo returned home to find out that the elephant had escaped with the ancestral spear. Labongo was enraged by this and demanded that Gipir retrieve the spear. Gipir pleaded with his brother to accept a replacement spear, but Labongo refused to accept anything but the same spear that he had sworn to guard with his life.

Labongo ordered his brother to find the spear and not to come back home without it. Gipir was gone for months, which led some to believe that Gipir may have been killed in the forest. Gipir had in fact found the dead elephant and retrieved the spear, but he was weary and sick from his journey. Gipir came upon an old woman in the forest who nursed him back to health. She gave Gipir food, new sandals, and some royal beads.

Gipir finally returned home. Women and children greeted him, but Gipir walked by them without even acknowledging them. He went straight to his brother to deliver the spear. Before Labongo could respond, Gipir stormed off in anger. Months went by after this incident and one day some of his family came to admire the royal beads that Gipir came back with. As he was threading the beads some of them fell to the ground and one of Labongo's daughters swallowed it.

Gipir brought the child to Labongo, demanding to have his beads back immediately. Labongo begged his brother to accept a replacement bead, but Gipir refused. Gipir also refused to wait until the girl had passed the beads out. Labongo immediately became ashamed when he remembered how he had ignored his brother's pleas months earlier. Labongo ordered that his daughter be cut open so that the beads could be removed. She died as a result of this. This incident eventually caused the separation of the two brothers.

It is this tragic tale that helped to shape the Luo understanding of justice and forgiveness. It was the inability of the two brothers to forgive each other that led to the tragic, but avoidable death of Labongo's daughter, so Mato Oput developed from the understanding that forgiveness and reconciliation are key elements to dealing with disputes and conflicts.

The first step in Mato Oput is truth telling, which is "rigorous, straightforward and transparent." Rev. MacBaker Ochola describes: "Through public confession, the offender community becomes vulnerable and guilty for the crimes committed by one of its members. This is the fundamental basis for community-based collective responsibility of the offender community."

The second step is that reparations are paid to the victims and survivors. The compensation is paid to demonstrate the sincerity of the offender. The next step is that the offender community and the offended community share food together. MacBaker Ochola explains that in the Luo community "sharing of food with one another is a fundamental fellowship." The fourth and final step is the drinking of bitter herbs, which is done to symbolize drinking up all the bitterness of the conflict. The bitter juice, which is obtained from an oput tree, is poured into a calabash and drank by selected participants.

For the final step in the process of Mato Oput, three or four representatives are selected to represent the community. In the selection process, an aunt must always be selected as one of the representatives. MacBaker Ochola gives the explanation that in Luo culture the aunt holds a special position in the family and that she has the final say in all matters relating to the family.

Revenge is justifiable in Luo culture, but only if the offender refuses to accept responsibility for their crime. The offender's refusal to accept responsibility is taken as a challenge to the community and in this situation the community has "lapir" or "just cause." The concept of revenge for unpunished crimes is so ingrained in Luo culture that there is a belief that if a person is killed by an unknown assailant, the victim will return as a vengeful spirit to get revenge against the murderer and the community in which the murderer lives.

Certain crimes were outside the realm of Mato Oput. For example, gang rape was not known among the Acholi, therefore Mato Oput did not cover such a crime. Other crimes that were not covered by Mato Oput were father-daughter incest and cannibalism. These crimes were so grave that they were attributed to the Ogre (Obibi), as such crimes went beyond normal humanity to the realm of the demons. Overall, the Acholi society was one where there was little theft or violence. Ochola explains:

Because of the Luo cultural and traditional prohibition of theft, the traditional Luo house had a very simple door called 'kikka' which was not burglar proof because there were no burglars in traditional Luo society. Kikka was not meant to keep out violence because traditional Luo society was non-violent. A child had no problem to enter a house since the kikka could easily be pulled either way, right or left. Kikka, therefore, was the symbol of a non-violent and peaceful community.

The people of Uganda decided to turn to Mato Oput to help resolve the damage caused by the conflict because there was simply nothing to be found within the Western colonial system which could address itself to the atrocities caused by the fighting, so Ugandans turned to a traditional system which was rooted in their own history and culture to find a solution for the problem.

Here, we shall offer on last example to further illustrate the point that history can be used to address contemporary challenges in Africa. Ntombi Dube, a health worker from Swaziland, argued: "There is no traditional life to live any more. It is sad that the old multi-generational homestead where women held respected roles is a thing of the past [...] We can't go back to that, and we have to adapt as African women who are proud of a culture that respects women. That respect got lost somewhere." Another women's activist from Swaziland named Cynthia Simelane made a similar case, stating: "All these laws that make Swazi women second-class human beings, they were not part of traditional Swazi life because we did not live under Western laws. Swazi women want to return to the way it was when we were equal." Simelane further argued that: "We are taking a page from the past to achieve the recognition Swazi women deserve as the ones who keep this society going."

These comments were made in light of the struggles that women have undergone in Swaziland. King Mswati III, who has been criticized for living a luxurious lifestyle while so many in Swaziland live in poverty, signed a new constitution which gave men and women equal rights in 2005. This has not prevented discriminatory laws, however, such as one that prevents women from taking out bank loans. Another law prevents women from owning property. As the statements from Dube and Simelane reflect, this type of treatment of women was not inherently rooted in traditional Swazi society. Here we see that a problem which traces its roots the colonial influence in Africa and the solution to the problem would be a return to traditional values which respect women. This again demonstrates the importance of African cultural values.

4 COLONIAL MIS-EDUCATION

Carter G. Woodson was among one of the earliest writers to document the impact of the miseducation of African people in his work *The Mis-Education of the Negro* (1933). In this book, Woodson noted that "Negroes are taught to admire the Hebrew, the Greek, the Latin and the Teuton and to despise the African." Woodson further explains:

> When a Negro has finished his education in our schools, then, he has been equipped to begin the life of an Americanized or Europeanized white man, but before he steps from the threshold of his alma mater he is told by his teachers that he must go back to his own people from whom he has been estranged by a vision of ideals which in his disillusionment he will realize that he cannot attain.

Woodson's essential argument in this book is that African people go to schools which alienate them from their own identity and condition them to be imitations of their European counterparts, which effectively alienates such educated Africans from their own people. Moreover, these educated Africans are then frustrated with the fact that certain barriers exist which prevent them from truly being Europeans, despite being trained to think and act as Europeans. Woodson also argues that before African people are physically lynched, they are mentally lynched in classrooms that help to reinforce their inferiority. Woodson considered the lynching that took place in the classroom to be the "worst sort of lynching" because it "kills one's aspirations and dooms him to vagabondage and crime."

Psychologists Kenneth Clark and Mamie Clark played a seminal role in the *Brown v. Board of Education* ruling which deemed segregated education to be unconstitutional. The Clarks conducted a test in which they had black children choose between a black doll and white doll. What they found was that the majority of black children preferred the white dolls. This test provided evidence that segregated education had a detrimental impact on the self-esteem of black children and this discovery played a seminal role in the decision by the Supreme Court to overturn segregation in schools. Forty years later when the doll test was repeated, the results were the same. Clark described the results as being "disturbing."

When the same test was conducted in Trinidad and Tobago it was shown that black children had an even stronger preference for the white dolls than did children in the United States. Elmo Gopaul, the secretary general of the Trinidad and Tobago teacher's union, responded by saying: "Even in Trinidad, where 85 percent of the people are black and we have a black government, we have not recovered from 400 years in which blacks knew the white man as the boss." So it is clear that the problem remained long after segregation in schools was ruled unconstitutional, and the issue even exists in nations where African people have never experienced segregated education. The implications of Clark's study were clear, but what was the solution to this problem? Clark's findings played a major role in the *Brown v. Board of Education* case, in which segregated schools were ruled unconstitutional, but tests afterwards have shown repeatedly that little progress has been made in terms of improving the self-esteem of black children.

So why is it that integrated schools were not the solution? The answer to this question lies in the fact that integration really does not get to the root of the self-esteem issues that face African children. Psychologist Asa G. Hilliard III (1978) explained:

> It must be remembered that the present push for "integrated education" had its roots in the general, belief that the education which most white children were getting was a quality education, *and* that if only Afro-American and other cultural groups could be present when this quality education was offered, they would be better off than under segregation.

The point that Hilliard was making here is that the fundamental mistake in the desegregation process was the idea that the education white people were receiving was superior. Therefore, the conclusion some came to was that by simply giving black children the same education it would improve their situation. Those who view the mere integration of schools as being a solution to the self-esteem issues of black children ignore the fact that black children did not face the same challenges that white children did, therefore they should not receive the same education. The doll test is a perfect example of this. If the black child was made to associate blackness with being ugly or unattractive, then the education that black children received should have been an education that would correct those distorted views, but no such education is to be found in the curriculum that white children received.

Rather than integrated education which taught African children the same thing that white children learned, African children should have been getting an African-centered education based on their own needs and historical experiences. It was mentioned earlier that when Clark's doll tests were conducted in Trinidad it produced similar results as in the United States, despite the fact that the government at the time was a black one. The reason for this can be found in the education that children in the Caribbean receive. Trinidadian born teacher and calypsonian Hollis Liverpool (1994) stated of the educational system in the British West Indies:

> Sad to say, too, students in the British Caribbean, especially those in history or music, know very little of the history of their music or of Latin American or even Afro-American history. Except for a few courses on Caribbean, African, and Latin American history and heritage available at the University of the West Indies, the culture of Africans in the wider African continuum (the Western Hemisphere, Africa, and Europe) is simply not taught. Yet the same students are exposed daily to European culture. Students in the U.S. Virgin Islands are better off, for at least they are exposed to U.S. and Afro-American history, but even that is limited. How then can Africans in the continuum appreciate and respect one another, or even learn of each other's existence?

What Liverpool is describing here is essentially the same education system that prevailed during the days of British colonial rule, in which West Indians were educated to become loyal British subjects. That system of education remained entrenched in the Caribbean even after independence was achieved. The issue in the educational system of the post-colonial Caribbean is that even after Africans gained political independence from Britain, the colonial education system remained and continued to have an adverse impact on the self-image of African children.

Thus we see a parallel between the educations of Africans in the Caribbean with that of Africans in the United States. In both cases African people managed to gain more political freedoms. Caribbean nations became independent and were free to develop themselves as they saw fit, but were unable to break away from Eurocentric models of education and governance because that is what they were educated—or rather trained—to do. In the United States the successes of the civil rights movement also did not address the miseducation that African Americans underwent. The failure of integrated education was the failure to break with this Eurocentric mentality.

We also see a similar phenomenon in Nigeria, which like Trinidad, was a former British colony. The Nigerian novelist Chinua Achebe recalled that one day his four year old daughter claimed, "I am not black; I am brown." Achebe decided to investigate where his daughter had acquired such a negative perception of being black and he discovered that the books that she had been reading were books that were imported from Europe. Such books depicted Africans in demeaning ways. This urged Achebe to begin writing children's books. The point here is that even in post-colonial Nigeria, African children were faced with negative depictions of African people on a regular basis. It is also worth noting here that Achebe's daughter was not being influenced by what she was learning in school, but through the European imported books that she was reading. This demonstrates that the struggle to educate African children is one that not only takes place in the classroom, but outside the classroom as well.

Marcus Garvey once declared: "Education is not so much the school that one has passed through, but the use one makes of that which he has learned." This is relevant in light of the fact that education has often been used as a tool against African people, and a tool used to alienate African people from possessing a strong sense of self. In other words, the "education" African people have received has been typically used in order to aid in the continuing exploitation of Africans. For this reason African people have to reassess our very concept and understanding of precisely what education is.

The contradiction that we often see with education is that the educated African is not educated to benefit the African community, but they are educated rather to maintain the oppression of African people or as Bobby E. Wright (1984) explained, "Black intellectual enlightenment does not always lead to genuine insight and it can be very damaging to the intellect as reflected by the behavior of many eminent Black scientists." What is even more problematic for African people is that it is often the mis-educated Africans who occupy leadership positions within the community, but their very education renders them ineffective as leaders of African people. In *Black Power*, by Kwame Ture and Charles Hamilton (1967), we are told about the educated black leadership in the United States:

> There has developed in this country an entire class of "captive leaders" in the black communities. These are black people with certain technical and administrative skills who could provide useful leadership roles in the black communities but do not because they have become beholden to the white power structure.

Therefore what we need is not so much education, but a particular type of education that will work to the benefit of African people. In the context of educating African children, the study of history is important for the mere fact that it provides a model for education. African people were not a people without a system of education or no desire for education. In fact, Walter Rodney (1969) tells us about the demand for books in Timbuktu:

> In a city which was renowned for its trade in gold, there was more profit to be made from books than from any other line of business! In other words, learning was valued more highly

than gold!

For the purposes of this topic, we will look briefly at how education functioned in Africa prior to European conquest. Prior to European colonization, African societies did have their own educational systems and these educational systems were part of the function of the society. The Yoruba, for example, viewed education as a lifelong process, and not something that was over when one graduated from school. Indeed, the African concept of education was that the person is constantly growing and constantly learning. Sharon Adetutu Omotoso (2010) states that the educated person in Africa is:

> One who is equipped to handle successfully the problems of living in an immediate and an extended family; who is well versed in the folk-lores and genealogies of the ancestors; who has some skills to handle minor health problems and where to obtain advice and help in major ones; who stands well with the ancestral spirits of the family and knows how to observe their worship; who has the ability to discharge social and political duties; who is wise and shrewd in judgement; who expresses self not in too many words but rather in proverbs and analogies leaving hearers to unravel his or her thought; who is self controlled under provocation, dignified in sorrow and restrained in success; and finally and most importantly, who is of excellent character.

Omotoso further states that: "While the Western conception of education is individualistic, the African conception of education is holistic; socially and functionally oriented. Both orientations have varying value. On a daily basis, Western individuality is eating deep into African societies; for instance, in recent marriages, communalism becomes a vice and the 'me and my wife syndrome' is raised above the traditional African communalistic style which used to exist." John K. Marah (2006) writes of the wisdom and knowledge that the griot possessed, stating:

In West Africa, there were griots 'walking dictionaries,' historians, or verbal artists who memorized the history, legends of a whole people and would recite them and teach their apprentices or audiences, publicly or privately; direct instruction was also employed.

Contributing to the holistic and community oriented feature of African education was a concept known as age-grades. Chancellor Williams (1987) described age grades as follows:

Age grades, sets, and classes are social, economic, political, and military systems for (1) basic and advanced traditional education (formal). (2) Individual and group responsibility roles. (3) Police and military training. (4) Division of labor. (5) Rites of passage and social activities. In chiefless societies the age grades are the organs of social, economic and political action.

Education in Africa was organized in a system of age grades, and what one learned was directly linked to which level of the age grade one belonged to. Children learned the basic necessities needed to deal with the challenges of society; which included being able to name certain plants and animals. As they grew older, they were given more specialized knowledge. This education was not only divided on age, but also on gender, thus young girls got a type of education that would prepare them for woman-hood. They were trained in childcare, cooking, social relations, and how to be successful wives and maintain an intimate relationship with their husbands.

We find that within African societies boys were educated in preparation for manhood and girls were educated in preparation for womanhood. This education was done through initiation societies. In Sierra Leone and Liberia, for example, there was the Poro society for boys and the Sande society for girls, which prepared boys and girls for adulthood. In *The Dark Child* (1945), Camara Laye describes the experience of being initiated in the bush schools of Guinea, stating:

The teaching we received in the bush, far from all prying eyes, had nothing very mysterious about it; nothing, I think, that was not fit for ears other than our own. These lessons, the same as had been taught to all who had preceded us, confined themselves to outlining what a man's conduct should be: we were to be absolutely straightforward, to cultivate all the virtues that go to make an honest man, to fulfill our duties toward God, toward our parents, our superiors and our neighbors. We must tell nothing of what we learned, either to women or to the uninitiated; neither were we to reveal any of the secret rites or circumcision. That is the custom. Women, too, are not allowed to tell anything about the rites of excision.

The society trained these children in preparation to function within the social order, including the family structure. It prepared them for adulthood and for life in the societies that they would grow up to live in. Breaking up the education into age grades was also a particularly useful way to acculturate these children by gradually preparing them for adulthood, but the age grade also served another function. David Conrad (2010) explains:

One of the main purposes of age grades is to provide a sense of social togetherness that goes beyond the family. This is why, when a Mande person who is away from home meets another Mande, she or he will introduce a fellow villager as a brother or sister.

The communal and holistic nature of education in African societies provides African children with advantages that children in Western societies do not demonstrate. Marcelle Geber noticed this when she tested three hundred babies in Uganda. She found that the infants there were superior to Western children when it came to psychological maturity, coordination, and language skills. Interestingly, Geber found that children of more educated parents were less mature than the babies of mothers that were uneducated. The key difference was that the uneducated mother had a stronger attachment to the child. Therefore, it is the family orientated and communal elements of traditional African society that contributed to the development of children to the point that they matured quicker than children living in more developed countries in the Western world.

This communal approach to education differs greatly with the more individual approach of Western education. One of the problems that we see pertaining to African people in the Western system of education is the failure to recognize the societal factors that also impact the lives of African children. It is as if African children are educated in a vacuum that is removed from the daily realities of racism, oppression, self-hate, and poverty. Instead, the educational system is often geared towards finding problems that are believed to be inherent within the African child, without also assessing problems within the social structure in which those African children live. Asa G. Hilliard points out:

> The real problem of racism and oppression in education is hidden too in the popular scholarship on the problem. Almost universally, scholarly studies of educational problems for minorities focus on the search for some deficit in the minority population, which will obviously require help from those who are "qualified to help." Almost totally absent from the theories and the practical work of scholars is any study of the dynamics and mechanics of racism and oppression.

In other words, the analysis of the problem of education for African children now moves away from the source of the struggles of African children and moves towards trying to find a deficit in their character or behavior. Thus the black child's behaviors are analyzed and scrutinized, and no attention is paid to the society in which that child lives and how the society itself shapes certain behaviors. This is not only a problem within the education system, but it is a problem that confronts psychology as a whole for when analyzing social problems some have made the mistake of focusing solely on the individual while neglecting the society that the individual lives in.

5 A LEGALLY CREATED PEOPLE

In *Psychopathic Racial Personality and Other Essays*, Bobby E. Wright argued that African Americans "are the world's only legally created group, (created through the 13th, 14th, and 15th amendments which can be repealed at any moment by the Congress or declared unconstitutional by the Supreme Court)." Wright's statement spoke to the very precarious legal situation which African Americans have been in. Congress has never repealed these amendments, but historically Congress has not consistently enforced the protections offered by these amendments. The Supreme Court has never declared the amendments unconstitutional, but the Supreme Court has certainly limited the protections offered by these amendments and has also limited the protections offered by civil rights legislation. In other words, Congress and the Supreme Court have not eliminated the legislation which was implemented to provide African Americans with the rights of citizenship, but such rights have been abridged so as to also protect the right of white people to discriminate as they see fit.

The Fourteenth Amendment was the amendment which provided citizenship for African Americans. The amendment reads:

> All persons born or naturalized in the United States, and subject to the jurisdiction thereof, are citizens of the United States and of the State wherein they reside. No State shall make or enforce any law which shall abridge the privileges or immunities of citizens of the United States; nor shall any State deprive any person of life, liberty, or property, without due process of law; nor deny to any person within its jurisdiction the equal protection of the laws.

The Fourteenth Amendment, in theory, provided equal status for African Americans. In practice, however, African Americans continued to endure racism and the deprivation of the rights which white citizens enjoyed. This has even included white immigrant groups who arrived in the United States after African Americans did. Although some European immigrant groups such as Italians and Irish did endure discrimination and prejudice in America, African Americans have been the group that has been consistently denied of their constitutional rights, to such an extent that it has required several amendments to the Constitution and the passage of civil right laws to protect the constitutional rights of African Americans; rights which are due to American citizens at birth.

Consider the fact that the Constitution itself had to be altered to provide more protections to African Americans. The Constitution had to be amended just so that persons of African descent who were born free in the United States could be regarded as being equal with white citizens. Consider the numerous civil rights bills that were passed for the purpose of providing equal treatment and equal protection to African Americans. This is what Bobby E. Wright referred to when he stated that African Americans were a legally created people. It took the alteration of American law for African Americans to be regarded as equals under that very law. This created a separate legal status for African Americans, which was much different from the legal status of white citizens.

The struggle to obtain equal citizenship rights must also be understood in economic terms as well because the exploitation of African Americans was not merely a form of racial oppression, but a form of economic oppression as well; a type of oppression which benefited the financial interests of white citizens. African people were dragged to the United States for the purpose of being enslaved. African people did not willingly go to America to be worked as slaves. Moreover, slavery was an industry which many individuals profited from. Slaves were a commodity, which were bought and sold on auction blocks. The slave also worked for the slave master without pay.

The primary reason why Africans were brought to the United States was to be utilized for slave labor. For this reason, when the United States was founded, the laws which were implemented were laws which were consistent with America's slave society. The laws were also consistent with the white supremacist views held by some of the Founding Fathers. Thomas Jefferson, for example, expressed the view that "the blacks, whether originally a distinct race, or made distinct by time and circumstances, are inferior to the whites in the endowments both of body and mind."

The United States was not formed with the interests and the well-being of African people being a central focus. This was so painfully true that despite the horrible conditions which enslaved Africans had to endure inside of the slave ships which brought them to America, the Constitution ensured that the slave trade would be protected until 1801. Article 1, Section 9, Clause 1 reads: "The Migration or Importation of such Persons as any of the States now existing shall think proper to admit, shall not be prohibited by the Congress prior to the Year one thousand eight hundred and eight, but a Tax or duty may be imposed on such Importation, not exceeding ten dollars for each Person."

Newly liberated Africans were now making the transition away from being commodities in a slave society to being laborers in a capitalistic society. Slavery itself had played a significant role in the development of Western capitalism. This is a point that Eric Williams documented in his book *Capitalism and Slavery*. Unlike slaves, the worker in a capitalistic system is not owned by a master. In the system of capitalism, a worker freely contracts to provide his or her laborer to an employer who pays the worker a wage in return for the worker's labor. Whereas a slave is made to work against his or her will—often through the threat of force—the worker is compelled to work because the worker needs to earn a wage in order to pay for necessities such as food and shelter.

In the relationship between the employer and the employee, the employer generally maintains the dominant position. One does not have to adhere to Karl Marx's theories to understand that within the system of capitalism contradictions between the worker and the employer can and do arise. Marx envisioned that the working class would one day rebel against the capitalist ruling class and that this revolution would bring forward a communist society in which the means of production are commonly owned by the workers themselves rather than being owned and controlled by a few capitalists who profit from the labor of the working class.

America was never subjected to the type of communist inspired revolution which Russia experienced, but America certainly has not been immune to struggles between the working class and the owners of the means of production. The dangers of unrestrained capitalism are precisely why Marx envisioned an eventual uprising on the part of the working class, which would overturn the exploitative capitalist system. Such a revolution may very well have been inevitable in industrialized capitalist countries if not for reforms and regulations which restrict the power of the employer and provide protections for the employee. Far from overturning a system in which the working class labors for wages, the reforms ensure that the working class is not overworked and underpaid. These regulations have also ensured that children cannot be employed to work as laborers and that workers can be compensated if they are injured while working.

African people found themselves oppressed not only within a society that implemented a very strict racial hierarchy, but also a system with a class hierarchy as well. It is for this reason that civil rights legislation can be understood to be not only about protecting African Americans from racial discrimination, but also about protecting working people from being exploited by their employers. After all, an African who was denied a job on account of his or her race was not only being discriminated against racially but was also a victim of a capitalist system which places the worker at the mercy of the employer. Again, one does not need to adhere to the theories of Marx to understand that in an economic system where one's survival is based on the ability to earn a wage from an employer, there is an inherent inequality that can be easily exploited to the benefit of the employer and to the detriment of the employee.

The Supreme Court has often struggled with maintaining the balance between allowing capitalists to freely engage in the pursuit of enriching themselves and regulating businesses for the purpose of protecting the interests of workers. Where the two interests clashed, there were times when the Supreme Court took the side of the capitalist employer over that of the worker. This was very apparent during the so-called Lochner Era. This era is so called because of *Lochner v. New York*, 198 U.S. 45 (1905), which was a case in which the Supreme Court struck down a New York state law that regulated the working hours of bakers. *Lochner* was one of several cases in which the Supreme Court struck down measures that were implemented to improve the conditions of American workers.

In *Lochner*, Justice Rufus Peckham, who delivered the opinion, declared that the "general right to make a contract in relation to his business is part of the liberty of the individual protected by the Fourteenth Amendment of the Federal Constitution." Justice Peckham continued to explain that the "right to purchase or to sell labor is part of the liberty protected by this amendment, unless there are circumstances which exclude the right." The Supreme Court in *Lochner* held that working hours for bakers was not one of those circumstances where the right to purchase and sell labor should be abridged. Justice Peckham explained: "There is no reasonable ground for interfering with the liberty of person or the right of free contract, by determining the hours of labor, in the occupation of a baker."

Justice Peckham cited *Holden v. Hardy*, 169 U.S. 366 (1989) which was a case in which the Supreme Court held that a law limiting the work hours of miners and smelters was a valid exercise of police power by the State, but Justice Peckham explained that the ruling in *Holden* did not apply in *Lochner*. Peckham explained that the law limiting the work hours of bakers was not related to protecting the safety of the bakers or the well-being of the public, as clean and wholesome "bread does not depend upon whether the baker works but ten hours per day or only sixty hours a week."

Peckham indicated that limiting the work hours of bakers was not as serious a concern as limiting the working hours of miners, but there was yet another issue that factored into the Supreme Court's ruling in *Lochner*. That issue was the power of the State versus the liberty of individuals. Justice Peckham explained as much when he framed the case as being "a question of which of two powers or rights shall prevail—the power of the State to legislate or the right of the individual to liberty of person and freedom of contract." In this case, the right of individual liberty and freedom of contract prevailed.

In *Lochner*, Peckham declared that "the liberty of contract relating to labor includes both parties to it. The one has as much right to purchase as the other to sell labor." The rights are not equal, however. In a capitalist economy, the party contracting for the purchase of labor typically has a number of advantages over the party contracting to sell his or her labor. A most obvious advantage is that the employee relies on the income he or she receives from the employer. For this reason, the employer is in a better position to dictate the terms of employment to the employee.

Yet another advantage which employers enjoy is the at-will doctrine, which allows an employer to discharge an employee for any reason at all. The Supreme Court of Alabama in *Allied Supply Co. v. Brown*, 585 So. 2d 33, 35 (Ala.1991) described the doctrine as thus: "Employees at will can terminate their employment, or can be terminated by their employer, at any time, with or without cause or justification." The Supreme Court of Alabama noted that the "at-will" doctrine has been criticized as being harsh, but that it remained the law in Alabama. The Supreme Court of Tennessee held in *Payne v. Western & Atlantic. R.R.*, 81 Tenn. (1884) that men "must be left, without interference to buy and sell where they please, and to discharge or retain employees at will for good cause or for no cause, or even for bad cause without thereby being guilty of an unlawful act per se."

The Supreme Court of Tennessee in *Payne* quoted Judge Cooley, who stated: "It is a part of every man's civil rights that he be at liberty to refuse business relations with any person whomsoever, whether the refusal rests upon reason, or is the result of whim, caprice, prejudice or malice. With his reasons neither the public nor third persons have any legal concern." The logic expressed by Cooley here is precisely the type of logic used to defend racial segregation. Under such reasoning, it would be the civil right of every man to deny business relations to an African American solely on the basis of prejudice and it would not be of any legal concern to the African American who is denied business relations.

Should racists be forced to contract with African Americans? Holding such a view necessarily entails that certain rights on the part of the racist individual will be curtailed or infringed upon. How far then can the law go to establish racial equality? How far should the law go? These are questions that must be asked in order to assess the role that legislation has played in attempting to resolve the problem of racial discrimination in the United States. Prior to the civil rights movement, courts adopted the view that the law must not go too far in imposing against the segregationist because doing so would infringe on one's freedom to reject engaging in business relations with whomever one pleases and for whatever reason one chooses.

There is also the question of whether or not it is practical for racial problems to be addressed through imposing racial integration against the will of the racists. The argument against this is not only that it infringes upon the rights of the racist, but that it would perhaps be better for African Americans to avoid being around racists who harbor such negative, bigoted, and hateful views. Perhaps it may be in the best interests of African Americans to avoid such racist individuals altogether. The problem with this approach is that racial separation in of itself is not a solution to the problem so long as rules which are designed to restrict the rights of African Americans remain in place.

As a minister of the Nation of Islam, Malcolm X drew a distinction between segregation and racial separation. In an interview with Eleanor Fischer, Malcolm X explained his views, stating: "Segregation is that which is forced upon an inferior by a superior. Separation is done voluntarily by two equals." Segregation was imposed upon African Americans. Segregation was the law and this law was implemented to enforce racial inequality.

What of separation? Malcolm X said that separation was done on a voluntary basis by two equals. The problem here is that there was an unequal relationship and for this reason African Americans were not free to build separately or independently from the dominant white society. The Nation of Islam preached a doctrine of racial separation. To achieve this vision of separation, Elijah Muhammad advocated the creation of a separate state for black people. The Nation of Islam was free to preach separation, but the Nation of Islam lacked the power or capacity to truly carry out this separation and the American government was certainly not going to give in to the Nation of Islam's demands for land to build a separate nation. The Republic of New Afrika also demanded land to create a separate black nation.

Just as those who struggled for integration were met with a backlash, the Nation of Islam and other black separatist organizations were met with a similar backlash. Segregation was the law. Any attempts at racial integration were therefore a violation of that law, yet the segregationists did not view the black separatists as being preferable to the integrationists. On the contrary, black nationalism and the doctrine of black separation was viewed as a threat because it was an assertion of African American independence. The entire purpose of segregation was to keep African Americans in their place; to keep African Americans oppressed and subjugated. Integration was a threat to the status quo, but assertions of African American independence were also a threat as well because it was contrary to the goal of keeping African Americans subjugated.

Due to the threat of African American independence, building separate institutions from white people has been a challenge because when African Americans have done so it has been perceived as competing against white interests and eliminated for this reason. Ida B. Wells-Barnett was a well-known anti-lynching activist whose activism was motivated by the fact that her friend Thomas Moss had been lynched because Moss opened a grocery store, which was seen as a threat to a nearby white owned grocery store. African Americans did not have the freedom to patronize white owned businesses, but African Americans could not open and operate their own businesses without facing discrimination either. Therefore, separation alone is not a solution so long as African people do not have the necessary protection from white aggression.

Now that the matter of racial segregation has been briefly addressed, we shall return again to the manner in which the Supreme Court ruled on labor issues during the Lochner Era. In 1919, the Congress passed the Child Labor Law tax which imposed a tax on companies which employed child labor. A furniture manufacturer known as the Drexel Furniture Company incurred a ten percent tax on its net profits for allowing a fourteen year old boy to work in its factories. In *Bailey v. Drexel Furniture Co.*, 259 U.S. 20 (1922), the Supreme Court held that this tax imposed on Drexel was unconstitutional.

President William Taft, who was then serving as the Chief Justice of the Supreme Court, explained that the Child Labor Law "is attacked on the ground that it is a regulation of the employment of child labor in the states—an exclusively state function under the federal Constitution and within the reservations of the Tenth Amendment." The Tenth Amendment provides that: "The powers not delegated to the United States by the Constitution, nor prohibited by it to the States, are reserved to the States respectively, or to the people." In other words, since the Constitution did not delegate to the United States the ability to restrict child labor and because the use of child labor was not prohibited to any of the states, the argument which was made against the Child Labor Tax was that it was a violation of states' rights.

The Supreme Court in this case held that the tax was unconstitutional because the taxes were in fact a penalty against businesses which utilized child labor. Taft explained that "a court must be blind not to see that the so-called tax is imposed to stop the employment of children within the age limits prescribed. Its prohibitory and regulatory effect and purpose are palpable. All others can see and understand this. How can we properly shut our minds to it?"

In *Coppage v. Kansas*, 236 U.S. 1 (1915), the Supreme Court held that it was legal for an employer to forbid an employee from joining a union. The plaintiff, Coppage, was found to be guilty of violating a state statute. Section one of that statute provided: "That it shall be unlawful for any individual or member of any firm, or any agent, officer, or employee of any company or corporation to coerce, require, demand, or influence any person or persons to enter into any agreement, either written or verbal, not to join or become or remain a member of any labor organization or association as a condition of such person or persons securing employment or continuing in the employment of such individual, firm, or corporation."

The purpose of the law was to bar employers from preventing their employees from joining unions, which was precisely what Coppage did. Hedges was employed as a switchman by the St.

Louis & San Francisco Railway Company. He was also a member of a labor organization called the Switchmen's Union of North America. Coppage was employed by the railway company as superintendent. Coppage requested Hedges to sign an agreement to withdraw from Switchmen's Union. Hedges was informed that if he did not sign it then he could not remain employed.

The Supreme Court held that the law enacted by the state of Kansas violated the "due process" clause of the Fourteenth Amendment. Justice Mahlon Pitney, who delivered the opinion, stated that "it is said by the Kansas Supreme Court (87 Kansas, p. 759) to be a matter of common knowledge that 'employees, as a rule, are not financially able to be as independent in making contracts for the sale of their labor as are employers in making contracts of purchase thereof.'" Of this inequality between employees and employers in making contracts, Justice Pitney remarked that "wherever the right of private property exists, there must and will be inequalities of fortune; and thus it naturally happens that parties negotiating about a contract are not equally unhampered by circumstances." Justice Pitney continued to explain that it is self-evident that "unless all things are held in common, some persons must have more property than others, it is from the nature of things impossible to uphold freedom of contract and the right of private property without at the same time recognizing as legitimate those inequalities of fortune that are the necessary result of the exercise of those rights."

Justice Pitney seemed to have been arguing that upholding freedom of contract and the right to private property cannot be done without also creating "inequalities of fortune", which are seen as the outcome of exercising such rights. Here one may ask whose freedom of contract and right to private property was the Supreme Court interested in protecting? If it would be a violation for a state to impose laws which bar employers from preventing employees from joining unions, would it not as equally be a violation of freedom of contract for employees to be barred from joining a union? The central issue being addressed by the Supreme Court was whether or not the freedom of contract of the employer should supersede that of the employee.

In the end, the Supreme Court held that it was not a significant infringement upon the right to freedom of contract of employees to allow employers to deny employees the ability to join a union. Justice Pitney explained that to "ask a man to agree, in advance, to refrain from affiliation with the union while retaining a certain position of employment, is not to ask him to give up any part of his constitutional freedom. He is free to decline the employment on those terms, just as the employer may decline to offer employment on any other; for 'It takes two to make a bargain.'" Justice Pitney continued to note that after having accepted employment under those terms, the employee is still free to join a union after the period of his employment ends.

An employee can, as Justice Pitney noted, either decline employment on those terms, which means trying to find employment elsewhere or the employee could merely join a union after the period of employment ends. The problem with such an approach is that if an employer is free to prevent employees from joining unions then the protections offered by the ability to unionize are nullified. There also is no guarantee that an employee will even find an employer who is willing to allow employees to join unions. The Supreme Court was effectively prioritizing the freedom of an employer to deny the right to unionize to its employees over the right of an employee to join a union.

Justice Oliver Holmes wrote a dissent to the Supreme Court's ruling in *Coppage*. Justice Holmes explained: "In present conditions a workman not unnaturally may believe that only by belonging to a union can he secure a contract that shall be fair to him. [...] If that belief, whether right or wrong, may be held by a reasonable man, it seems to me that it may be enforced by law in order to establish the equality of position between the parties in which liberty of contract begins."

Holmes concluded his dissent by writing: "I therefore think that the statute of Kansas, sustained by the Supreme Court of the State, did not go beyond a legitimate exercise of the police power, when it sought, not to require one man to employ another against his will, but to put limitations upon the sacrifice of rights which one man may exact from another as a condition of employment. Entertaining these views, I am constrained to dissent from the judgment in this case."

These rulings by the Supreme Court demonstrated the conflict between a laissez-faire approach which allows businesses to do as they please and the ability of the government to regulate businesses to avoid the harsher aspects of the capitalist system. These cases also demonstrated the tensions between protecting the rights of workers, while also protecting the right to freedom of contract of the employers. As was already noted, unrestrained capitalism can be very harsh for workers, who are given very little protection from exploitation. It is for this reason that states had to enact policies to protect workers through placing regulations on employers. Relying on the good-will of the employers was simply not enough, especially when the employers had a financial incentive to exploit workers.

Federal regulations and restrictions were especially required to protect African Americans, who not only required employee protections, but racial protections as well. This is also relevant to the point mentioned previously about African Americans being a legally created people. The rights offered to American citizens in the Constitution were not rights that were readily extended to African Americans. Instead, African Americans needed separate laws merely just to be recognized as citizens and to enjoy constitutional rights, such as liberty to contact.

After the aforementioned Lochner Era, the Supreme Court began to rule in favor of regulations and restrictions. The National Labor Relations Act of 1935 was passed to allow employees the ability to unionize without interference from the employer. This legislation was ruled to be constitutional by the Supreme Court in *National Labor Relations Board v. Jones & Laughlin Steel Corporation*, 301 U.S. 1 (1937). The Supreme Court held:

That is a fundamental right. Employees have as clear a right to organize and select their representatives for lawful purposes as the respondent has to organize its business and select its own officers and agents. Discrimination and coercion to prevent the free exercise of the right of employees to self-organization and representation is a proper subject for condemnation by competent legislative authority. Long ago we stated the reason for labor organizations. We said that they were organized out of the necessities of the situation; that a single employee was helpless in dealing with an employer; that he was dependent ordinarily on his daily wage for the maintenance of himself and family; that if the employer refused to pay him the wages that he thought fair, he was nevertheless unable to leave the employ and resist arbitrary and unfair treatment; that union was essential to give laborers opportunity to deal on an equality with their employer.

In *West Coast Hotel Co. v. Parrish*, 300 U.S. 379 (1937), the Supreme Court ruled in favor of establishing a minimum wage for laborers. In this case, Elsie Parrish, who was employed as a chambermaid, brought a suit to recover the difference between the wages paid to her and the minimum wage fixed pursuant to the Washington state law, which set minimum wage at $14.50 per week of 48 hours. Chief Justice Charles Hughes explained:

In each case the violation alleged by those attacking minimum wage regulation for women is deprivation of freedom of contract. What is this freedom? The Constitution does not speak of freedom of contract. It speaks of liberty and prohibits the deprivation of liberty without due process of law. In prohibiting that deprivation the Constitution does not recognize an absolute and uncontrollable liberty. Liberty in each of its phases has its history and connotation.

Chief Justice Hughes also explained that the "essential limitation of liberty in general governs freedom of contract in particular." Given that the liberty to contract is not absolute, the Supreme Court does have the ability to restrict freedom of contract. In this particular case, the Supreme Court decided that freedom of contract does not prevent states from enacting regulations to protect workers. Chief Justice Hughes mentions a number of regulations which had been implemented, such as an eight-hour work day for underground miners and smelters, forbidding the payment of seamen's wages in advance, and maintaining workmen's compensation laws. Chief Justice Hughes explained that "the legislature has necessarily a wide field of discretion in order that there may be suitable protection of health and safety, and that peace and good order may be promoted through regulations designed to insure wholesome conditions of work and freedom from oppression."

The Supreme Court was also concerned with protecting workers from undue economic exploitation because when workers are denied a living wage, it is taxpayers who are made to pay the cost of living for those workers:

There is an additional and compelling con-sideration which recent economic experience has brought into a strong light. The exploitation of a class of workers who are in an unequal position with respect to bargaining power, and are thus relatively defenceless against the denial of a living wage, is not only detrimental to their health and wellbeing, but casts a direct burden for their support upon the community. What these workers lose in wages, the taxpayers are called upon to pay. The bare cost of living must be met.

The Supreme Court's ruling in *West Coast Hotel Co.* demonstrated that protecting workers meant limiting freedom of contract for employers. One of the fundamental principles in contract law is "freedom of contract." This refers to the freedom of persons to enter into contracts. It must be made clear that a contract is not merely an agreement between parties. A contract is a legally binding agreement and therefore the party which breaches the contract can be found to be legally liable for the breach. Contract law is based on the principle that one should be held accountable for the promises that one makes to others. Of course, not every promise is regarded by the courts as being a contract. Indeed, a contract refers to a very specific type of promise, consisting of three elements: an offer, acceptance, and consideration.

The Supreme Court held in *Dred Scott v. Sandford*, 60 U.S. (19 How.) 393 (1857) that Africans were not regarded as American citizens, regardless of if they were enslaved or freed. As such, the rights that were offered to American citizens were not enjoyed by African people. Enslaved Africans were regarded as chattel or property, which could be bought, sold, or traded. Freedom of contract meant the freedom to enter into contracts for the sale of enslaved persons. Owning an enslaved African was a property right for which the Constitution granted protection. Article IV, Section 2, Clause 3 of the Constitution reads:

> No person held to service or labour in one state, under the laws thereof, escaping into another, shall, in consequence of any law or regulation therein, be discharged from such service or labor, but shall be delivered up on claim of the party to whom such service or labour may be due.

The word slave is not used in the clause, but the effect of the clause was obviously meant to ensure that slave masters had the right to have their property returned to them if that property were to escape. The right to private property protected the right of slave masters to own Africans. Much like other forms of property, banks were able to acquire a secured interest in slaves. Enslaved Africans were used as collateral for loans which were issued by banks and when borrowers defaulted on their loans, banks were able to take ownership over the slaves.

The struggles that African Americans continued to endure after the abolition of slavery was in many ways a struggle for freedom of contract. The racial segregation which followed the abolition of slavery was aimed at restricting the ability of African Americans to exercise freedom of contract. This struggle was clearly illustrated in *Civil Rights Cases*, 109 U.S. 3 (1883), which were cases that were brought before the Supreme Court regarding the first and second sections of a civil rights act which was passed by Congress on March 1, 1875, entitled "An Act to protect all citizens in their civil and legal rights."

The plaintiffs, in five cases from lower courts, were bringing suits alleging civil rights violations. The claims included denying to persons of color the accommodations and privileges of an inn and denying to individuals the privileges and accommodations of a theatre, along with other claims. In delivering the opinion of the Supreme Court, Justice Joseph Bradley explained: "The essence of the law is, not to declare broadly that all persons shall be entitled to the full and equal enjoyment of the accommodations, advantages, facilities, and privileges of inns, public conveyances, and theaters; but that such enjoyment shall not be subject to any conditions applicable only to citizens of a particular race or color, or who had been in a previous condition of servitude."

Congress' power to enact civil rights legislation rests in the Fourteenth Amendment, which stipulates that "no State shall make or enforce any law which shall abridge the privileges or immunities of citizens of the United States; nor shall any State deprive any person of life, liberty, or property without due process of law; nor deny to any person within its jurisdiction the equal protection of the laws." Justice Bradley explained that there was no question that the Fourteenth Amendment "nullifies and makes void all State legislation, and State action of every kind, which impairs the privileges and immunities of citizens of the United States, or which injures them in life, liberty, or property without due process of law, or which denies to any of them the equal protection of the laws."

Bradley explained that the Fourteenth Amendment "does not invest Congress with power to legislate upon subjects which are within the domain of State legislation; but to provide modes of relief against State legislation, or State action, of the kind referred to." Justice Bradley continued to explain that the Fourteenth Amendment "does not authorize Congress to create a code of municipal law for the regulation of private rights; but to provide modes of redress against the operation of State laws, and the action of State officers, executive or judicial, when these are subversive of the fundamental rights specified in the amendment." Bradley concluded that "until some State law has been passed, or some State action through its officers or agents has been taken, adverse to the rights of citizens sought to be protected by the Fourteenth Amendment, no legislation of the United States under said amendment, nor any proceeding under such legislation, can be called into activity: for the prohibitions of the amendment are against State laws and acts done under State authority."

In *Civil Rights Cases*, the Supreme Court, in essence, held that private citizens have the right to engage in racial segregation and that the Fourteenth Amendment does not authorize Congress to regulate the actions of private citizens who choose to discriminate on the basis of race. The problem with such an interpretation is that it severely limited the enforcement of the Fourteenth Amendment by allowing individuals to discriminate. More so than this, however, the Supreme Court ruling held that individuals could deny African Americans the freedom to contract. This will be addressed in more detail, but the point to be made here is that the Supreme Court ruling in *Civil Right Cases* undermined important pieces of legislation which were intended to ensure that African Americans were protected from discrimination, as well as given equal treatment and opportunities under the law.

Yet another problem that arises from interpreting the Fourteenth Amendment is what constitutes due process? This is important because the Fourteenth Amendment provides, as previously noted, that no "State shall make or enforce any law which shall abridge the privileges or immunities of citizens of the United States; nor shall any State deprive any person of life, liberty, or property, without due process of law; nor deny to any person within its jurisdiction the equal protection of the laws." The Fourteenth Amendment protects citizens against the arbitrary deprivation of rights and privileges, but what happens when the deprivation of such rights and privileges are written into the law and upheld by the courts? At this point the citizen is no longer being deprived of any rights without due process because the law itself enforces such deprivation of those rights.

In *Plessy v. Ferguson*, 163 U.S. 537 (1896), the Supreme Court stated, "we think the enforced separation of the races, as applied to the internal commerce of the State, neither abridges the privileges or immunities of the colored man, deprives him of his property without due process of law, nor denies him the equal protection of the laws, within the meaning of the Fourteenth Amendment [...]." The Supreme Court here was willing to permit racial segregation, stating that enforced separation of the races was not depriving an individual of the right of due process.

The laws were not so straightforward as to outright ban African Americans from voting because of their racial identity. Instead, the voting restrictions appeared to be racially neutral on their face. This included policies such as a poll tax, which required voters to pay a tax in order to register to vote. On its face a poll tax appears racially neutral. In fact, poll taxes have historically barred white citizens from voting just as it has barred black citizens, but the "grandfather clause" was one of the means by which white citizens could escape the requirement of a poll tax. The grandfather clause exempted individuals who were able to vote prior to January 1, 1867, or individuals who were the son or grandson of an individual who could vote prior to that time. Prior to 1867, African Americans were not eligible to vote in Louisiana and for this reason the grandfather clause would not apply.

In *Louisiana v. United States*, 380 U.S. 145 (1965), the Supreme Court held that Louisiana's voter restriction policies were unconstitutional. In 1921, Louisiana replaced the grandfather clause with an "interpretation test" which required an applicant for registration to "give a reasonable interpretation" of any clause in Louisiana's Constitution or the Constitution of the United States. From the adoption of the 1921 interpretation test until 1944, African Americans never exceeded one percent of the registered voting population. Prior to 1944, African Americans only had a slight interest in voting since Louisiana's laws prevented African Americans from voting in the Democratic Party primary election. Justice Hugo Black, who delivered the opinion of the Court, noted that the Supreme Court had previously invalidated an identical primary law in Texas in *Smith v. Allwright*, 321 U.S. 649 (1944).

Black noted that the white primary system had so effectively barred African Americans from voting that the "interpretation test" as a device for disenfranchisement was ignored. Due to an increase in the number of registered African American voters and the 1954 Supreme Court decision which invalidated the laws upholding school segregation, Louisiana sought new ways to bar African Americans from voting. A "Segregation Committee" was created by the Louisiana Legislature for this purpose.

In *Harman v. Forssenius*, 380 U.S. 528 (1965), the Supreme Court held that Virginia's voter registration policies were unconstitutional. Virginia eliminated the poll tax requirement for federal elections and substituted a provision in which the federal voter could qualify either by paying the customary poll tax or by filing a certificate of residence six months before the election. The Supreme Court held that these new restrictions which were implemented by Virginia were in violation of the Twenty-fourth Amendment.

The poll tax in Virginia was implemented for the purpose of preventing African Americans from being able to vote. There was no secret about this at all. At the Virginia Constitutional Convention of 1902, the sponsor of the suffrage plan in which the poll tax was included, stated very frankly: "Discrimination! Why, that is precisely what we propose; that, exactly, is what this Convention was elected for—to discriminate to the very extremity of permissible action under the limitations of the Federal Constitution, with a view to the elimination of every negro voter who can be gotten rid of, legally, without materially impairing the numerical strength of the white electorate." This statement, which was delivered by Carter Glass, is very revealing not only because it demonstrated that there was no pretense about denying African Americans the ability to vote, but also because it demonstrated that racist legislators were trying to discriminate as much as they could within the limits of the Constitution.

In *Harper v. Virginia Board of Elections*, 383 U.S. 663 (1966), the Supreme Court overturned the prior ruling in *Breedlove v. Suttles*, 302 U.S. 277 (1937) holding that poll taxes violated the Equal Protection Clause of the Fourteenth Amendment and were therefore unconstitutional. In his dissent, Justice Hugo Black wrote that the Court's decision was "to no extent based on a finding that the Virginia law as written or as applied is being used as a device or mechanism to deny Negro citizens of Virginia the right to vote on account of their color." Black explained that if "the record could support a finding that the law as written or applied has such an effect, the law would of course be unconstitutional as a violation of the Fourteenth and Fifteenth Amendments and also 42 U. S. C. § 1971 (a)." Black appeared to disagree with the Court's ruling "that the Equal Protection Clause necessarily bars all States from making payment of a state tax, any tax, a prerequisite to voting." In Black's view *Breedlove* was correctly decided because the "mere fact that a law results in treating some groups differently from others does not, of course, automatically amount to a violation of the Equal Protection Clause."

The Voting Rights Act of 1965 was passed to enforce the voting rights provisions of the Fifteenth Amendment. The second section of the Fifteenth Amendment gave Congress the power to enforce the Fifteenth Amendment through passing the appropriate legislation, although it took pressure from the civil rights movement for Congress to finally pass legislation to protect the voting rights of African Americans. Merely just being citizens should have guaranteed African Americans equal voting rights under the law, but this was not the case. The very purpose for implementing the Fifteenth Amendment was to protect the voting rights of African Americans, but even then, additional legislation was needed to protect those voting rights.

Justice Harlan's dissent in *Civil Rights Cases* helped to highlight how selective the Supreme Court has been with which rights it has chosen to enforce. Harlan stated that "the substance and spirit of the recent amendments of the Constitution have been sacrificed by a subtle and ingenious verbal criticism." Harlan also explained "that the court has departed from the familiar rule requiring, in the interpretation of constitutional provisions, that full, effect be given to the intent with which they were adopted." Harlan continued to explain: "The purpose of the first section of the act of Congress of March 1, 1875, was to prevent *race* discrimination in respect of the accommodations and facilities of inns, public conveyances, and places of public amusement."

Justice Harlan took issue with the fact that the Supreme Court's ruling in the case was contrary to the intent with which the Fourteenth Amendment was adopted. Justice Harlan explained that section 2, article IV of the Constitution gave Congress the authority to pass the Fugitive Slave Law of 1793, which established "a mode for the recovery of fugitive slaves, and prescribing a penalty against any person who should knowingly and willingly obstruct or hinder the master, his agent, or attorney, in seizing, arresting, and recovering the fugitive, or who should rescue the fugitive from him, or who should harbor or conceal the slave after notice that he was a fugitive."

Justice Harlan's reference to the Fugitive Slave clause of the Constitution is noteworthy here because it demonstrated that the Supreme Court was willing to uphold the right of slave masters to retain control over their slaves, but the Supreme Court was much less willing to enforce constitutional measures which were designed to prevent racial discrimination. Justice Harlan noted that "the Constitution recognized the master's right of property in his fugitive slave, and, as incidental thereto, the right of seizing and recovering him, regardless of any State law, or regulation, or local custom whatsoever" and that "the right of the master to have his slave, thus escaping, delivered up on claim, being guaranteed by the Constitution, the fair implication was that the national government was clothed with appropriate authority and functions to enforce it."

Justice Harlan noted that the constitutionality of the Fugitive Slave Act of 1850, much like the Fugitive Slave Law of 1973, rested "solely upon the implied power of Congress to enforce the master's rights." Harlan continues to note that these provisions "placed at the disposal of the master seeking to recover his fugitive slave, substantially the whole power of the nation." Justice Harlan's dissent rightfully pointed out that the American judicial system found no problem with enforcing constitutional provisions which protected the right of a slave master to maintain enslaved persons as property. Fugitive slave provisions were meant to ensure that individuals who no longer wished to be enslaved had no say in the matter. Such individuals were forcibly returned if they ran away. When it came to the Fourteenth Amendment, there was much less willingness on the part of the judicial system to enforce the protections which the Constitution offered to African Americans. Fugitive slave provisions benefited slave masters, even if doing so was against the desire of the enslaved. Similarly, the Supreme Court's willingness to uphold segregation benefited racist segregationists, against the desires of those who were excluded because of these segregationist policies.

The willingness to enforce the Fugitive Slave Clause in the Constitution was demonstrated in *Prigg v. Pennsylvania*, 41 U.S. (16 Pet.) 539 (1842), which was another Supreme Court case. Edward Prigg was a citizen of Maryland who was indicted in Pennsylvania for kidnapping Margaret Morgan, an African woman who was born into slavery and escaped to Pennsylvania. Under the laws of Maryland, Morgan was a slave for life to her master,

Margaret Ashmore. Prigg tracked down and captured Morgan in Pennsylvania for the purpose of returning Morgan into slavery.

By the time of this case Pennsylvania had already abolished slavery. The act which outlawed slavery stated: "All persons, as well negroes and mulattoes, as others, who shall be born within this state, shall not be deemed and considered as servants for life or slaves; and all servitude for life, or slavery of children, in consequence of slavery of their mothers, in the case of all children born within this state, from and after the passing of this act as aforesaid, shall be and hereby is utterly taken away, extinguished and for ever abolished."

The Pennsylvania law which Prigg was charged with violating stated:

If any person or persons shall, from and after the passing of this act, by force and violence, take and carry away, or cause to be taken or carried away, and shall, by fraud or false pretence, seduce, or cause to be seduced, or shall attempt so to take, carry away or seduce, any negro or mulatto, from any part or parts of this commonwealth, to any other place or places whatsoever, out of this common-wealth, with a design and intention of selling and disposing of, or of causing to be sold, or of keeping and detaining, or of causing to be kept and detained, such negro or mulatto, as a slave or servant for life, or for any term whatsoever, every such person or persons, his or their aiders or abettors, shall on conviction thereof, in any court of this commonwealth having competent jurisdiction, be deemed guilty of a felony, and shall forfeit and pay, at the discretion of the court passing the sentence, a sum not less than five hundred, nor more than one thousand dollars, one-half whereof shall be paid to the person or persons who shall prosecute for the same, and the other half to this commonwealth; and moreover, shall be sentenced to undergo a servitude for any term or terms not less than seven years, nor exceeding twenty-one years, and shall be confined and kept to hard labor, fed and clothed in the manner as is directed by the penal laws of this commonwealth for persons convicted of robbery.

The Supreme Court ultimately reversed the conviction of Prigg, holding that "under and in virtue of the Constitution, the owner of a slave is clothed with entire authority, in every state in the Union, to seize and recapture his slave, whenever he can do it without any breach of the peace, or any illegal violence." The Supreme Court concluded that the act of "Pennsylvania upon which this indictment is founded, is unconstitutional and void. It purports to punish as a public offence against that state, the very act of seizing and removing a slave by his master, which the Constitution of the United States was designed to justify and uphold."

Another issue raised in Harlan's dissent in *Civil Rights Cases* is whether or not inns can legally exclude individuals. Harlan quotes Justice Coleridge, who explained: "The innkeeper is not to select his guests. He has no right to say to one, you shall come to my inn, and to another you shall not, as every one coming and conducting himself in a proper manner has a right to be received; and for this purpose innkeepers are a sort of public servants, they having in return a kind of privilege of entertaining travellers and supplying them with what they want." Based on this, Harlan concluded that the public nature of an innkeeper's employment "forbids him from discriminating against any person asking admission as a guest on account of the race or color of that person."

The ruling in *Civil Rights Cases* was indicative of the fact that although legislation had been put in place to protect African Americans from racial discrimination, the Supreme Court tended to narrowly interpret these policies. As has been previously demonstrated, the justification for doing so was that a broad interpretation of such legislation would violate the rights of private citizens, who have the right to exclude people on the basis of race. The Supreme Court in *Civil Rights Cases* interpreted the Fourteenth Amendment to apply to State acts, as opposed to the acts of private citizens.

The maintenance of segregated facilities was justified by the "separate but equal" doctrine put forward by the Supreme Court in *Plessy*. This doctrine was successfully challenged in *Brown v. Board of Education of Topeka*, 347 U.S. 483 (1954), in which the Supreme Court held that the separate but equal doctrine could not apply to public schools because "[s]eparate educational facilities are inherently unequal." The Supreme Court further held "that the plaintiffs and others similarly situated for whom the actions have been brought are, by reason of the segregation complained of, deprived of the equal protection of the laws guaranteed by the Fourteenth Amendment."

Apart from the argument to be made about the equal quality of facilities which was addressed in *Brown*, there is also the question of equality of liberty. All American citizens should have the same protections and the same rights under the law. This should mean that public facilities which are open to white people should be just as much open and available to African Americans. Unfortunately, even after the Fourteenth Amendment granted African Americans citizenship, citizenship did not mean equality under the law. In *Brown*, the Supreme Court finally decided to hold that segregation was a violation of the Constitution.

The ruling in *Brown* was a blow against segregation, but it was also a blow to black educators as well. Bobby E. Wright explained that "as a result of the 'infamous' 1954 school desegregation decision, Blacks have lost an estimated 35,000 teaching and administrative positions in the South. Former Black principals of Black schools are now janitors in integrated schools and the same thing is going to happen to Black teachers in the North."

There is also the matter of freedom of contract, which was discussed previously in the context of employment. The Supreme Court wrestled with where to draw the limit to the freedom of contract in the context of employment. The Supreme Court was in the position of trying to balance the necessity of protecting workers, while also preserving the liberties of employers. This balance becomes even more complicated when one introduces the variable of race. Not only is there a question of protecting the workers while minimally intruding upon the rights of employers, but also the question of protecting African American workers from racial discrimination, given that at one point freedom of contract also meant freedom to discriminate on the basis of race.

Freedom of contract meant that a white employer had the freedom to deny an African American solely on the basis of race. This meant the denial of things such as employment, rent, or, denial of service, to give but a few examples. This was perfectly legal under American law prior to the abolition of slavery. There were no provisions which guarded against racial discrimination in the process of contract formation and African Americans were not regarded as being citizens. African Americans were regarded as property and, as already noted, freedom of contract meant the freedom to buy and sell that property; the freedom to buy and sell Africans. Africans were the subject of contracts but did not have any legally protected rights to freely engage in contracts for their own benefit.

The Civil Rights Act of 1866, which was passed after the abolition of slavery, finally addressed the problem regarding the lack of protection for African Americans in regard to making contracts. The 1866 act not only made African people citizens under American law, but it provided freedom of contract to all citizens. Section 1981 of the 1866 Civil Rights Act provides:

All persons within the jurisdiction of the United States shall have the same right in every State and Territory to make and enforce contracts, to sue, be parties, give evidence, and to the full and equal benefit of all laws and proceedings for the security of persons and property as is enjoyed by white citizens, and shall be subject to like punishment, pains, penalties, taxes, licenses, and exactions of every kind, and to no other.

In theory, African Americans were just as free as white citizens to make and enforce contracts, but in practice there was still no equality. This is demonstrated by Jim Crow laws, which barred African Americans from accessing the same facilities as white people. This also included housing and employment discrimination, which adversely impacted the ability of African Americans to find shelter and to earn a living. This was the very thing which the Civil Rights Act of 1866 was meant to prevent, but, as was typically the case with legislation that was meant to prevent racial discrimination, the Supreme Court applied a very narrow view regarding when such protections against racial discrimination applied.

Patterson v. McLean Credit Union, 491 U.S. 164 (1989) offers an example of the Supreme Court's very narrow approach to interpreting the protections offered by § 1981. Brenda Patterson, an African American woman, was employed by McLean Credit Union as a teller and a file coordinator. After being laid off in 1982, Patterson commenced a suit against her former employer. She alleged that Mclean Credit Union, in violation of 14 Stat. 27, 42 U.S.C. § 1981, had harassed her, failed to promote her to an intermediate accounting clerk position, and then discharged her because of her race. Patterson also claimed this conduct amounted to an intentional infliction of emotional distress, actionable under North Carolina tort law. The District Court determined that a claim for racial harassment is not actionable under § 1981 and declined to submit that part of the case to the jury.

The Supreme Court held that Patterson did not have a claim under § 1981, given that the scope of this statute prohibited the "mak[ing] and enforce[ment]" of contracts alone. Based on the language of § 1981, Justice Anthony Kennedy explained: "Where an alleged act of discrimination does not involve the impairment of one of these specific rights, § 1981 provides no relief. Section 1981 cannot be construed as a general proscription of racial discrimination in all aspects of contract relations, for it expressly prohibits discrimination only in the making and enforcement of contracts." The Supreme Court ultimately held that Patterson's claim was not actionable under § 1981 because the conduct which she alleged was not related to the formation of the contract.

Peterson alleged that she was subjected to various forms of racial harassment from her supervisor. This included being periodically stared at for several minutes at a time; being given too many tasks, which led to her complaining that she was under too much pressure; the tasks that she was given were sweeping and dusting tasks which were not given to white employees; and she also alleged that she was passed over for promotion. Justice Kennedy explained that with "the exception perhaps of her claim that respondent refused to promote her to a position as an accountant [...] none of the conduct which petitioner alleges as part of the racial harassment against her involves either a refusal to make a contract with her or the impairment of her ability to enforce her established contract rights." Justice Kennedy also explained: "Interpreting § 1981 to cover post-formation conduct unrelated to an employee's right to enforce his or her contract, such as incidents relating to the conditions of employment, is not only inconsistent with that statute's limitation to the making and enforcement of contracts, but would also undermine the detailed and well crafted procedures for conciliation and resolution of Title VII claims."

The Supreme Court's ruling in *Patterson v. McLean Credit Union* held that § 1981 does not apply to discrimination which occurs after the contract has been formed. In other words, § 1981 ensures that African Americans have the freedom to enter into employment contracts, but are not protected from being discriminated against after being employed. Based on this interpretation, § 1981 does not offer unlimited protection against racial discrimination and employers are free to discriminate, just so long as they do so after the contract has been formed, at least where § 1981 is concerned. The other statute which provides protection against employment discrimination is Title VII.

The passage of the Civil Rights Act of 1964 was a landmark moment in the civil rights movement and one of the provisions of this act was Title VII. Title VII of the Civil Rights Act of 1964 prohibits employers from discriminating against employees on the basis of race, color, religion, sex or national origin. Since the passage of the Civil Rights Act of 1964, the Supreme Court has, on more than one occasion, ruled in ways which would make it more difficult for employees to prevail under Title VII or Title VII related claims. One example of this was the ruling in *Price Waterhouse v. Hopkins*, 490 U.S. 228 (1989). Ann Hopkins brought a lawsuit against her employer, Price Waterhouse, alleging sex discrimination pursuant to Title VII. Hopkins was the only female candidate proposed for partnership in 1982 out of the eighty-eight persons proposed for partnership. She was denied the partnership and alleged that she was discriminated against on the basis of her sex.

The partners in Hopkins' office praised her character as well as her accomplishments, but Hopkins was also known for her abrasive behavior. Hopkins' poor interpersonal skills ultimately doomed her bid for partnership. Despite her professional success and strong qualities, Hopkins was described as being "sometimes overly aggressive, unduly harsh, difficult to work with, and impatient with staff."

The Supreme Court noted that there was evidence to demonstrate that some partners reacted strongly to Hopkins' behavior because she was a woman. She was described as being "macho" and another partner suggested that she "overcompensated for being a woman". Several partners criticized her use of profanity. One partner suggested that those partners objected to her swearing only "because it's a lady using foul language." Hopkins was told that if she wanted to improve her chances she had to "walk more femininely, talk more femininely, dress more femininely, wear make-up, have her hair styled, and wear jewelry."

Based on the facts of the case, Price Waterhouse did have legitimate concerns about Hopkins' interpersonal skills, which were assessed when determining whether or not to make her a partner. Yet, much of the negative response to Hopkins' behavior was based on sex stereotyping. The problem was not merely Hopkins' behavior, but that the partners believed that it was improper for a woman to behave in the manner that she was behaving. For this reason, one of the questions addressed by the Supreme Court in this case was whether or not Hopkins could still prevail on her sexual discrimination claim, despite the fact that Price Waterhouse articulated a legitimate reason for why Hopkins was denied partnership.

The Supreme Court looked at the language of Title VII, which prohibited an employer from making an adverse decision against an employee "because of such individual's . . . sex." The Supreme Court concluded that the phrase "because of" in Title VII meant "but-for causation." Justice Brennan concluded that in "determining whether a particular factor was a but-for cause of a given event, we begin by assuming that that factor was present at the time of the event, and then ask whether, even if that factor had been absent, the event nevertheless would have transpired in the same way."

This ruling meant that a defendant could escape liability if the defendant is able to prove that but for the alleged discrimination, the plaintiff would not have suffered an adverse employment action—examples of an adverse employment action include being discharged, demoted, or denied for a position. Brennan explained that "once a plaintiff in a Title VII case shows that gender played a motivating part in an employment decision, the defendant may avoid a finding of liability only by proving that it would have made the same decision even if it had not allowed gender to play such a role." In *Price Waterhouse*, the defendant merely needed to demonstrate that Hopkins would have still been denied for partnership even if her gender did not play a motivating factor. The ruling in *Price Waterhouse* allowed defendants to escape liability through proving that a legitimate reason motivated the employment decision, even if race, gender, religion, or other classes protected under Title VII were taken into consideration as well, while also imposing a higher standard for plaintiffs to meet in order to prevail in Title VII cases. Though *Price Waterhouse* was a gender discrimination case, the ruling also applied to racial discrimination cases under Title VII as well.

Congress passed the Civil Rights Act of 1991, which overturned the Supreme Court's narrow interpretation of Title VII in *Price Waterhouse*. Section 107(a) of the 1991 Civil Rights Act Amendment provides that an "unlawful employment practice is established when the complaining party demonstrates that race, color, religion, sex, or national origin was a motivating factor for any employment practice, even though other factors motivated the practice."

The 1991 civil rights bill made it easier for plaintiffs to prevail in Title VII discrimination cases by overturning the "but-for" requirement which the Supreme Court imposed in *Price Waterhouse*. The Supreme Court ruled, however, that a but-for causation analysis applied to retaliation cases, even if such cases arose out of an alleged violation of Title VII. The Supreme Court made this ruling in *University of Texas Southwestern Medical Center v. Nassar*, 570 U.S. 338 (2013).

Dr. Naiel Nassar, a physician of Middle Eastern descent who was both a University faculty member and a hospital staff physician, claimed that Dr. Levine, one of his supervisors at the University, was biased against him on account of his religion and ethnic heritage. Nassar complained to Dr. Fitz, Levine's supervisor, but after he arranged to continue working at the hospital without also being on the University's faculty, he resigned from his teaching post and sent a letter to Fitz and others, stating that he was leaving because of Dr. Levine's harassment.

Nassar filed a suit alleging Title VII violations. The first claim was a status-based discrimination claim under §2000e–2(a), claiming that Dr. Levine's racially and religiously motivated harassment resulted in his constructive discharge from the University. The second claim was that Dr. Fitz's effort to prevent the hospital from hiring him was in retaliation for complaining about Dr. Levine's harassment, in violation of §2000e–3(a).

Regarding Nassar's retaliation claim, the Supreme Court addressed the question of whether or not the lessened causation standard applied by Congress' statutory amendment to the Civil Rights Act of 1964 applied to retaliation claims. Justice Anthony Kennedy stated of the new standard imposed by Congress' 1991 act: "An employee who alleges status-based discrimination under Title VII need not show that the causal link between injury and wrong is so close that the injury would not have occurred but for the act. So-called but-for causation is not the test. It suffices instead to show that the motive to discriminate was one of the employer's motives, even if the employer also had other, lawful motives that were causative in the employer's decision." Justice Kennedy explained that prior to *Nassar*, the Supreme Court had not addressed the question of the causation showing required to establish liability for a Title VII retaliation claim. For this reason, the Supreme Court relied on its prior ruling in *Gross v. FBL Financial Services, Inc.*, 557 U.S. 167 (2009).

In *Gross*, the Supreme Court held that the Age Discrimination in Employment Act of 1967 (ADEA) required that the plaintiff prove that the plaintiff's age was the but-for cause of the prohibited conduct, much like the standard set by the Supreme Court in *Price Waterhouse*. The ADEA provides that "'[i]t shall be unlawful for an employer . . . to fail or refuse to hire or to discharge any individual or otherwise discriminate against any individual with respect to his compensation, terms, conditions, or privileges of employment, because of such individual's age.'" The Supreme Court held that the "because of" phrase in the ADEA meant that a but-for standard applied to the ADEA. Therefore, for a plaintiff to prevail in an ADEA claim, the plaintiff must demonstrate but for the plaintiff's age, the defendant would have not engaged in the adverse employment action. This also means that a defendant can escape liability by demonstrating that there was a non-discriminatory, legitimate reason for why the action was taken.

The Supreme Court noted that the ruling in *Gross* was instructive in the case of *Nassar*. Moreover, Justice Kennedy noted that "Title VII's antiretaliation provision, which is set forth in §2000e–3(a), appears in a different section from Title VII's ban on status-based discrimination." For this reason, the Supreme Court did not apply the 1991 act by Congress. Title VII's retaliation provision provides: "It shall be an unlawful employment practice for an employer to discriminate against any of his employees . . . because he has opposed any practice made an unlawful employment practice by this subchapter, or because he has made a charge, testified, assisted, or participated in any manner in an investigation, proceeding, or hearing under this subchapter."

The Supreme Court applied a "but-for" causation standard to Title VII's retaliation provision. This meant that although employment discrimination claims which arose under Title VII no longer required a "but-for" standard, if an employer were to retaliate against an employee for complaining about discrimination, the employee would have to meet the "but-for" standard set by the Supreme Court. As explained before, the Supreme Court applies the "but-for" standard due to the language of Title VII, but this interpretation of the language of Title VII is one which frustrates the very goal which Title VII was meant to accomplish.

For African people, becoming equal citizens and enjoying the rights which are guaranteed to an American citizen under the Constitution required an extensive overhaul of America's laws, but even then struggles persisted as many of these laws were not strictly enforced and it, as has been demonstrated, the Supreme Court often interpreted these laws in such a manner as to diminish the ability of these laws to protect African Americans from the very racial discrimination which the laws were designed to prohibit. Wright referred to African Americans as a legally created people because of the fact that legislation had to be implemented in order for African Americans to become citizens, but even with this legislation in place, the legal rights of African Americans continue to be held in a very precarious balance.